BY EDDIE GIBBONS

COLLECTIONS:

Stations of the Heart (Thirsty Books, 1999)
The Republic of Ted (Thirsty Books, 2003)
Game On! (Thirsty Books, 2006 – reprinted 2009)

ACKNOWLEDGEMENTS

Some of these poems first appeared in the following:
Unsuitable Companions (Happenstance Press, 2007)
Three-Way Street (Koo Press, 2004)
Zugzwang (Koo Press, 2002)

Thanks to the editors of the following:
Quadrant; Painted, spoken; Northwords Now;
    Textualities; Poetry Scotland; Pushing Out The Boat;
    Spring Tides; Aberdeen Writers' Circle Magazine;
    One Night Stanzas.

For Barbara and Jennifer

What They Say About You
Eddie Gibbons

Leamington Books 2010

Leamington Books Ltd. 3 Bothwell Street, Glasgow,
G2 6TS. Printed by Cromwell Press Group. Designed and
typeset by Gerry Hillman in Calisto Mt.

What They Say About You

CONTENTS:

EPILOGUE

The last poet on the planet
felt the weight of the word
upon him. Burdened with nouns,
shackled to adjectives, he could not
utter a sentence that was not laden
with meaning.

His wife and children had left him
because he could not say the words
bread, butter, knife,
without alluding to texture,
weather, the angle of light.

Children chided him, who spoke
such strange vocab: his convo-
luted diction, his strange Slavonic
vowels: he who spoke no logo-language.

And so the world shunned him, shied
away from his descriptions, became a place
of things, of that-which-is-pointed-at.

Wearied, he packed all his metaphors for
moon : *sun* : *stars* : *sky* : *time*
into a suitcase, and called it a day.

DECLARATION

After giving so-and-so a piece
of my mind, a few well-chosen
unkind words: a few uncivil assertions,
one or two inaccurate versions
of the goings-on i.e. chicanery,
shenanigans, a soupçon of devilry,
the circumventing of the facts,
the reinventing of the rights and wrongs,
I left him scolded, ear-bashed, lambasted,
then hitched a lift to the airport,
where the easyJet check-in girl asked
if I was carrying any sharp objects,
to which I declared – *only my tongue.*

DEATH SHALL HAVE NO DIM ONION

Shopping by woods this snowy eve,
I wonder why each word I read
gets muddled up, goes quite mad.
How did my eyesight get so bad?

Did Robert Browsing's Duchess go
not Gentile Into That Good Night?
Was Robert Frosty in the snow?
Is 'Tyger Tyger *burping*' right?

Poor Percy Shelley's really Pysshe
and Homer wrote the *Ilibad*.
Could Morgenstern recite his *Fish*?
Are Vasco Popadoms a fad?

Once Allen Ginseng's primal *Owl*
drowned out the waving Stevie Sniff
but *Hiya Watha*! makes me scowl
like Ruddy Kipling's iffy *If*.

Of all the joys of Muddle Age
myopia must head the queue.
I have to squint to read this page –
The Raver (Edgar Allen Poo).

IN PLACE OF POEMS

I recall my teacher asking the class
to write a poem about one of their relatives,
then for homework paint a picture of that person.
She called the lesson *Show and Tell*.

I dipped my nib in the inkwell, scrawled
a spiderweb of lines, then blotted my copybook.
At home I coloured in a drawing of my dad
going to work on his bike, sandwiches in his saddlebag.

Tonight, I'll step outside this page and hand to you
items that stood for poems in his world –
a *Football Echo*, bicycle clips, a clock-in card;
a freshly-machined cog dripping with soluble oil.

EVERY SINGLE DAY

In the Mall at Runcorn Shopping City, strangers
approach us – *You're Ted's kids, aren't you?*
I smile at being called a kid, Yvonne answers *Yes.*

He's a lovely bloke, your Dad –
I often speak to him down the Legion.
Tell him Margot was asking after him.

Everywhere we go, from Argos to Tesco's,
the same thoughts are echoed by passers-by;
Give him my best. God bless. I'll try to visit him soon.

Such kindness could make you weep when you think
this is happening every day to someone somewhere,
except for the wafer-thin grannies huddled

in cardigans and nighties at the hospital entrance
for fear of being alone – *I've got three kids.*
They never visit, never phone.

As I pass I clutch my bunch of flowers tight,
turn towards the stairs to his ward and think
This is hard. This is right.

GENESIS & TINNITUS

In The Beginning
was the First Word.

A man heard it.

In The End
was the Last Word.
A woman had it.

IN BED WITH ANGELA MERKEL

I watched Angela Merkel reading
When Saturday Comes in a Potzdamer Platz Café.

She was wearing a little black, red
and gold off-the-Schroeder number.

I heard her chanting softly:
Helmut Kohl scores own goal.
Helmut Kohl scores own goal.

I asked in imperfect Deutsch if the seat next to her
was vacant. She replied in perfect Scouse that it was.

Ich liebe you long time, I said to her. And I meant it.
I started humming *Angie* by the Rolling Stones,

like everyone who ever meets her does. She loves it.
I then recited in its entirety her entry in Wikipedia,

including all links, selected published works and trivia.
She was impressed. But then she's German.

I then confessed consuming jealousy over her Dubya
Bush massage and how it scandalized my heart –

how dare he touch my bunny Bundeskanzlerin –
the cuddliest German Chancellor in a month of Sonntags.

I made her promise to take me to G7 heaven.
I vowed not to sing *The Birdie Song* and act like

a Schlager lout, as usual. But I secretly plotted
to strangle George W with the braces of my Lederhosen.

When she invited me to tea at her flat on Einbahnstrasse
for Wiener Schnitzel, Schnapps and a penalty shoot-out

I shouted: *Let's reunify RIGHT NOW!*
You Schnukiputzi, you!

She offered little opposition.
We formed a coalition.

BECAUSE I AM A POET

I didn't wake at the clock's alarm.
I waited for the glorious dawn
to shake the shackles of sleep from my wrists.

At breakfast I weighed the Sugar Puffs
against the bacon but opted for the irony
of scrambled eggs and chicken soup.

After calculating the Centre of Gravity
of the rainbow outside my window, I devised
a formula for finding the avoirdupois mass
of any given teardrop.

Whilst doodling in the margins of a poem
by Wislawa Szymborska I recalled how once
I divined the alchemy of loss on your lips,
sharp as styptic on my tongue,
and fell in love with the Polish word
STĘSKNIONY.

Because I am a poet I know what rhymes
with *Oranjeboom.* I know the precise
chemical composition of Love Hearts.

I also know what *onomatopoeia, dénouement*
and *oxymoronic* mean, though I seldom use them
more than once in any given haiku.

After an evening training young verses
how to find their own voices, I stalk moonlit
paths into deep dark woods to recapture
fierce feral poems and herd them home
to their paper cages.

BUDDHA'S GIRLFRIEND

Sits in the shadow of a temple. Her name is Shirley.
It's 533 BC and 80 degrees in the shade.

Shirley sucks a lemonade and gazes at Siddhartha,
the man who stole her heart, a bloke who she calls *Sid*.

But all this Buddha biz is getting on her tits,
unlike her boyfriend. It's depriving her of sleep.

If he would only keep a single date,
stay out late, get stoned, legless, laid,

instead of sitting in the shade of the one-ton temple bell
thinking of moon moths. Hell, when will he get a life?

Oh, yes, his wife suspects nothing.
She's at home, ironing a billion wrinkled lotus petals.

Rishis chanting Vedic verses have more fun than Shirl
Has he noticed she's a girl? How tight her red dress clings?

His spiritual pursuits have really cramped his style.
If just once he'd take her dancing without her even asking.

If only once he'd send a Valentine, buy her roses,
chocolates, wine her in the Dharma Disco Bar,

fumble in her bra, give her tender kisses,
(she'd show him what bliss is!) but all he does is sit there.

Not that he doesn't care, but he's a one-ton temple bell
and she's a moth who might as well be on the moon.

ONCE UPON A TIME PIECE

I enter the House of Clocks
and reset each one a minute
behind its predecessor.

I exit an hour later, an hour earlier
than when I came in, to find
you haven't left me after all.

I wouldn't try this at home –
certain things can only happen in poems.

NIGHT WRITING

A shadow prowls night's outer edge.
How close it is I cannot say.
It's either at my window ledge
or it's a thousand beats away.

My landscape once again is white,
for stalking is a winter's task;
to print my markings for the sight
of others who stray from the pack.

I wander in the darker woods,
the trackless ground of mysteries,
where from imagination floods
such lives, such dreams, such histories.

I hunt, as those with spear or gun,
in this internal wilderness.
I'll hunt until my task is done
or I am killed by loneliness.

This recognition braces me.
I hear a distant howl, and pause.
I note a strange affinity
in this saliva at my jaws.

STRAFING

If love got on the bus
and asked me where I get off,

if it offered me a bite of its half-time pie,
or leaned on the bar and slurred in my ear,
I might just have an inkling of who it was.

If love came knocking on my door
I'd hide behind the sofa,
thinking it was the rent man.

If love arrived breathless,
years too late, I'd whisper:
I'm sorry, I'm no longer at this address.

But if love thundered like a Tornado
and bombarded my house, leaving me
dishevelled in the wreckage,
I'd know then that it really was love,
and I'd adopt the Solo Missionary Position
as that Tornado turned
and screamed along its strafing run.

WORD FOR WINDOWS

On the estate where I grew up
we didn't have neighbours,
we had witnesses.

And though we weren't unkind,
we robbed each other blind.

Some divvy stole my bike,
so I nicked someone else's.
It was a kind of bartering –
stealing like-for-like.

All through my adolescence
I learnt about the essence of living –
it's a game of give and take,
so I gave as good as I got.

The word on the street was GIVE WAY
so I gave way, but I didn't give in.

We were at that awkward age between
puberty and the pub, between
hopscotch and scotch on the rocks.

Although our diction seldom stretched
to triple syllables, our tongues were razors
that rendered language blunt.

Rozzers, teachers, neighbours bore the brunt.

If we gave our word we'd batter you,
our word was good.

And we had a word for windows –
that word was *wood.*

HEART EXHAUST

They are testing me for CAD
(Coronary Artery Disease).

Phase one is the stress scan.
This calls for a *trocar* and a *cannula,*
then a thump of *thallium* and a ribbon of
radio-active tracer into the myocardium.
Nothing hurts. I'm numb as a cadaver.

The nurses chat across the leaden hulk of me:

There's a slant on the graph, just there.
What does that mean?

It's going upwards so it means
the patient has probably already
had a heart attack. Is that not so, sir?

Not to my knowledge, I reply,
though I'm no expert in these matters.
You should consult a doctor.

The Kwik Fit Fitter takes a gander
at my car's exhaust pipe. The gattling
sound had alarmed me in the hospital car
park. Barely ambulant, the motor made it
to the garage, rattling the neighbourhood
with its barks and rasps. The fitter shakes
his head and gives me a mournful look.

What's the damage?
I ask.

AT THE JACQUES BOUTIQUE

Fashion?

The golden-gened wear it, are it.
The young declare it essential:
the very essence of pubescence.

Newspapers flog it
to death on each page,
raging against the crime of age.

If you don't fit it, fix it
with Atkins, Slim Fast or Detox –
suck the Lypo out of your buttocks.

Whatever you lack, implant it.
Youth? Decant it as a cream or spray.
Cure yourself with a Botox injection:

age is youth with a nasty infection.

THE ELECTRODE LESS TRAVELLED

The tall blonde Swedish girl points to my trousers
and orders: *Get Them Off!* So I get them off.

I am told to lie down and think of Ulrika.
(She doesn't really say that but it's what I do).

She sticks needles up and down my legs.
I have to compare each tiny pain to every other.

I'm wired with electrodes that send electric pulses
from the nerves in my feet, up my spine and back again.

If I shock you too much you can sue me for abuse –
so shout when the pain becomes unbearable.

I check that her badge reads NHS NEUROLOGY,
not GUANTANAMO BAY RENDITION CENTRE.

The readings I'm getting seem to suggest that
there might be an underlying non-neurological problem.
I think you will need to see your doctor for a blood test.
Also, it will help if you provide a urine sample.

I mull this over.

Let me get this straight – you're getting on my nerves
and now you want my doctor to take the piss?

So, what's left for my friends to do?

THE DOWNSIDE OF KNOWING A POET

Don't write.
Don't phone.
Don't wait
outside my door in the rain.

Yes, I adore you.
I'd do anything for you,

except ever see you again.

Your sorrow
is so tangible
I can taste it,

but our last parting
was so perfect,
it would be a shame to waste it.

HELPLESS

Your daughter's born. She is helpless.
You teach, you nurture, give her toys.
You bandage cuts and mend the breaks.

Years pass. Your child grows up. It takes
the blink of an eye. She meets boys
in clubs and falls in love. Helpless.

She goes on dates and graduates.
You cling to all the hard-won joys.
Your daughter's gone. You're helpless.

ENGLISH FOR FOREIGN FOOTBALLERS

Situation / Position / Condition

The **situation** is said to be lost
if your volley flies past the post.
A similar **condition** occurs
in any game featuring Spurs.

If caught way out of **position**
show a great deal of contrition-
say to your mates: *it's me modelling dates
that keep me out of* **condition.**

The Manager's heart **condition**
is caused by our league **position.**
His **situation** will only worsen
when he meets the chairman in person.

One FA Cup tradition,
to even the competition,
is a Premier team's demolition
by inferior opposition
who win by grit and ambition
and the pitch's appalling **condition**

Our latest acquisition
has this contract **condition:**
*The club will hang you for treason
if we don't win the League this season.*

You'll be in the Sundays, sport,
front page of every edition,
if you and that bimbo are caught
in a compromising **position.**

YOUTHEMISMS

i)
The roach in the ashtray
was the sign of a wasted youth.

ii)
The young are always in style.
They wear themselves so well.

iii)
Aracnephobia: fear of teenage spiders.

iv)
Stop patronising me, Dad.

vi)
Why do you never answer my questions?
Why do you always question my answers?

STANDING OUTSIDE THE BERG ROOM IN NEW YORK PUBLIC LIBRARY, HAVING BEEN REFUSED ENTRY, I CONTEMPLATE THE WORKS OF PAUL VIOLI

I risked arrest to stand here outside the locked door,
having upset the Black Lady Police Officer
with my enquiry as to where the Berg
(*that's B-E-R-G*) Room was located.

Ah can read,
Ah can write,
Ah can spell,
she retorted, her trigger-finger twitching.

I quickly explained that the previous person I'd asked
that question of thought I wanted the *bathroom,* hence
my spelling out the word.

She smiled the smile of the suffraghetto and pointed
with her still-twitching finger to the spot
where I now stand,

and will remain standing, having been politely
refused entry on the grounds that I was *A Dumb
Englishman*, and what would I know
about American Literature?

Nothing, evidently, my having asked of Mr. Violi
the previous evening if he'd had A BOOK published.

He smiled the smile of the Suffrajet-lagged, and,
painfully aware that he was confronted by *A Very Dumb
Englishman,* graciously replied that, yes, he'd had
A BOOK published, (modestly omitting the other ten).

Now, outside THE BERG, shamed by my ignorance,
I contemplate my options –

a) Try to appear as if I'm really a dumb *Scotsman.*

b) Break down the door and let all the books fly away.

c) Shout – *I got Paul Violi's autograph by threatening
to bore him to death*!

Realising that I have actually shouted c) out loud
and the Black Lady Police Officer has adopted
the *Nutcase in Library* firing position, I run to the Exit,
screaming misheard quotes from Mr. Violi –

*Lozenge nearly rhymes with Orange!
There are seven typists of ambiguity!*

10:29 Attempts to call Trace abandoned!

I hit the street, hollering-

Three across: *Dumb* is to *Englishman* as *Fruitcake* is to?

Eighty-Nine Down: What is the builder curious about?

Seven Up: Where do I bring fifty thousand in cash to?

Mad as a Bison berserk on Madison, I froth, I bark,
I howl until I tilt headfirst into the headlines –

*B-E-R-G ROOM EXCLUDEE ARRESTED
FOR RANDOM ACTS OF VIOLIENCE.*

A CALENDAR MONTH

It was a shock, entering the hut
where the electrician kept his voltmeters.
A jolt to glance at the current calendar
where a girl was smiling and waving
from beneath a jacked-up car.

Miss March, apparently a mechanic by trade,
would be followed later by Miss May, a valet,
and Miss June, a pump attendant, whose names
are as old-fashioned as April, whose showers
have seldom seen so many soft-focus soap suds.

August may be wicked, but July is a month
of sundaes. Here, a girl is driving a Citroën
Cabriolet through St. Tropez, ice cream in hand,
her honey blonde hair fluttering a Gendarme's heart.

Only Miss February, freezing at a petrol pump
with just a bobble hat to protect her from a blizzard,
is thankful for her shorter exposure, standing static
for the electrician, whose warm hands turned her over.

YEATS SHOOTS AND LEAVES

I will sit down and stay now, and stay and watch TV,
and a small pasty eat here which has been microwaved.
A bean can will I open to have with chips for tea.
I'll dine alone in the TV's gaze.

And I shall take my ease there, for ease I will lie low.
Drowsing from Real Ales in the morning
to watch the cricket swings.

At midday is my dinner, at twelve the burgers glow
and evening's full of the Tennent's tins.

I will sit down and stay now for it's *Home and Away*.
I hear their flip-flops flapping with low sounds
by the shore. While I lie on my deckchair
they pass and say *G'day*.

I answer with my TV snore.

A DIAMOND IN THE DISTRICT

Diamond Way, a glittering air.
Over there is where the woman
in Marathon Man shouted
Der Weisse Engel! at Szell.

Soaked Hasidics bemoan the pearls
of rain in their beards. One speaks
of carats to his mobile phone.

The street hums its mantra –
Sell! Sell! Sell!
Sidewalks teem with ermine stoles.
Windows gleam with stellar troves.
The dollar umbrella I bought
has rusted after three blocks' use.

I step into the doorway
of the Gotham Book Mart,
a shanty shack in this gleaming
street, and stand agape
at photographs of luminaries
signing books after ancient readings –
Auden, Lowell, Cummings, Jarrell.

I mine the poetry section
and find a hidden jewel –
a second-hand First Edition
of Berryman's *Dream Songs*.
Fifty dollars flat. Would Henry
be amused by that,
Mr. Bones?

Stepping back to the sidewalks
of the newly-dry Manhattan,
I ditch my useless umbrella
and head towards Madison,
toying with the rest of my dreams.

BUNKU

bun is soft, half baked
and likes to be buttered up –
is often toasted

bun runs yellow with
the sunburst of a burst sun –
eggy rivulets

the current bun is
fresher than the older one –
that's far too crusty

eggy buns induce
such discombobulation –
blue dress, yellow blobs

three writers composed
this triple-rasher poem –
me, bacon, bunyan

superpowers heed
this global warming warning –
iced buns are melting

antoinette repels
proletariat revolt –
then let them eat buns!

small profit margins
the baker's accountant asks –
is there dough in buns?

OUT OF THE BLUE

A dead hawk's ruby fluids poured
in dwindling streams across the moor.

In turmoil from the sky it bowled,
a heart too grave for air to hold.

A long shriek where the hawk had swooned.
A beak had burst the day's balloon.

A figure with a rifle stooped
to nail that last unruly swoop.

UTTERLY

For *Cannabis*, refer to *Smoke*.
For *Awake!*, witness *Jehovah*.
For *Fluff*, contemplate *Navel*.
For *Wondrous*, survey *Cross*.
For *Borrow*, check out *Desk*.
For *Trains*, observe *Closely*.
For *Worcester*, ask *Jeeves*.
For *Narcissus*, regard *Self*.
For *Monroe*, look up *Skirt*.
For *Rhythm*, scan *Shone*.
For *Gitanes*, see *Garret*.
For *Churchill*, see *Gare*.
For *Milton*, cite *Gonne*.
For *Raleigh*, see *Dog*.
For *Hitler*, see *Guile*.

THUS SPRACH ZEBEDEE

Time for bed!
It's sixty past ten.
Switch off your head,
start snoring again.
Wind up the cat.
Kick out the clock.
Climb into your pit
through the hole in your sock.
First set the telly to TV-am.
Draw the curtains in pencil or pen.
Shoot out the lights.
Switch on the dark.
Muzzle the kids
so they don't bark.
Tell them that fairies
give them three wishes.

You have the sex –
I'll do the dishes.

YOU'VE BEEN FRAMED?

You think you've been framed?
Someone's got it in for you?
Look at it from my point of view –

you didn't eat with a silver spoon, but you ate.
You never had two pennies to rub together,
but that single penny bought you plenty.
The bath was cold, the milk was warm,

all your clothes had been worn by someone
else before. The pipes froze, the tap leaked.
There was always a draft from the door.
Your shoes squeaked and the rain seeped
through the holes in your soles.

The boils on you neck hurt like heck
and the nit-comb scraped your scalp.
Your mum wasn't mean with the iodine
when she swabbed your open sores.
If you crossed your father it was hell
and leather and welts

that weeped for a week. Then an extra treat
from the headmaster – the cane for giving cheek.
The cock of the school had a golden rule: look
at me and you're dead. Through your childhood
years your main career was falling over:
you tripped, you hurt, you bled.

But listen up, before you start to blub
again: all that pain was the common coin
from the public purse. You got your money's worth,
that's all. So curse all you like – you wanted
for nothing and that's what you got.

Stitched? Set up? Framed?
You ought to be ashamed.

ON NOT RUNNING OVER A FOX OR A DEER
ON A LONELY ROAD AT NIGHT

Dammit!
Missed it!

Another poem
bites the dust.

UMBRAGE

When I said
Lie back and think of England
I'd forgotten you were Scottish.

So I said
Lie back and think of Britain.
Surely we're both British?

You said
Who d'ye think yer kiddin
wi this British *pish?*

Then the seething room went silent
except for a hiss
and the skean dhu's swish.

LIVERPOOL ECHOES

Passing an alley in a foreign town,
the wind seems to whistle a shanty.
A tang of salt coats my tongue.

A building looks the image of
the Bluecoat Chambers. I spot
an Adelphi, a Gambier, a Goree.

A dockside crane wire twangs
that first wild chord of *A Hard Day's
Night* and kick-starts my heart.

A poster shows a Matador razor-
sharp inside the swirl of his cape.
I recall a man in a pub saying:

*Your father must have been hard
as nails to grow up in The Bullring
tenements, son. They were brutal.*

My futile attempt at a foreign phrase
brings whoops of laughter: now that's
the language I learned from my father

when trams clanked down to the Pier Head,
the big ship sailed down the alley alley-o
and the Sons of Spion sang *ee-aye-addio:*

when I played football with Rory Storm
as Astrid Kirchherr shot the Beatles
in a basement on the Reeperbahn,

while the Quarrymen laboured at the rock face
of their ordinary lives, and that mad bastard Lennon
was let loose amongst the footlights and the headlines.

EPMTY NOW GRWOS ERVEY BED

Waht ocne was dnoe
is now udnone.
Waht ocne was naer
is far aawy.
And lvoe taht leightd
on yuor shuodler
in smoe ditsant Jnue
or May, has litfed now
and fittled swkyard,
out of viison,
folwn aawy.

Who ocne was hree
is now ewlshere.
The oen who hled
yuor seepling haed
now hlods antoher's
in its sumblers
in smoe dastint twon
intsead. Lkie haerts
and hoesus, cirbs
and craelds, eptmy
now grwos ervey bed.

ABYSSAL

Years pass in unremembered days, then this –
your lips are startled by a stranger's kiss –
someone you've been waiting for for years,
who has a searching look and knowing eyes.

All longings from the past melt with the kiss.
A hand is touched with tenderness, and this
arouses feelings drowned in arid years,
which rise by provocation of her eyes.

The wanton invitation in her eyes
belies the meaning of that modest kiss.
The signals sent are clouded by the years
you've needed to know happiness like this.

Be wary of those notions held for years,
and cautious of that step beyond a kiss.
You'll fall into the abyss of her eyes
and know no greater hopelessness than this.

MAGNUM HOPELESS

My uncle owned an ice cream van
in the days before the Mafia franchises.

I whipped up a price list for him
with crayons thick as Cadbury's Flakes.

At the age of nine my penmanship
became famous throughout the streets
of our tarmac-melting, sweltering estate.

Living in an area known as *The Poets*
I suppose I was predisposed
to a career in writin' –

(Huyton, Huyton, two dogs fightin'
one's a black and one's a white 'un)

My Magnum Opus
was displayed to all the kids in
Cowper Way –
        Shelley Close –
                Tennyson Avenue –

And many mouths would water in
Byron,
Burns &
Keats
as they read my creamy list.

For months on end I was
The Emperor of Ice Cream.

My words were heralded by chimes,
read with relish, consumed with joy.

I'll never be as famous as I was as a boy.

IN THE GREEN ROOM

For Alison Dunne, Robert Guzder and Michael Donaghy

She's washing dinner dishes
as we sit at the kitchen table.
Robert's leafing through her
copy of *Remembering Dances
Learned Last Night.*

All the time she's talking to us –

*Remember the Green Room
at the Bloomsbury?
How we scoffed those sarnies?
Guzzled that wine?*

We'll drink this one for Michael,
Alison says, and pours three neat
Armagnacs into crystal glasses.

Ah, yes, I think, that's how
I'll always remember the two of you-
calm before the reading:
you, thrilled and slightly tipsy,
twirling strands of your hair as you spoke;

and Michael standing behind you, a shy
and gentle man, looking like a refugee
from some exiled orchestra, searching
for the safest place to practise his flute.

NOTES FROM THE HURRYING MAN
For Brian Patten

I might have brushed against you, coming out of Blacklers,
where Pete Best's mother, Mona, bought him his first
drum kit. You, fresh from the Kardomah, seeking out
a scarf to shield you from the winter weather.

I might have brushed against the book of poems in your hand:
may have heard the distant howl of Ginsberg from L.A.,
or faintly glimpsed the city lights that shone on Ferlinghetti,
garaging his car in a downbeat Frisco low-rise.

You sipped Kardomah coffee with the icons of the Sixties.
I went to Kirkby Tech, along with other factory fodder.
I spent that decade dwalming in a muddled fug. The days
spun out like swarf, swift and jagged from my Boxford.

Yet, thirty years later, we shared a pint of blether –
talked about your mother, talked about my father
and the closing down of Blacklers. Then we stepped
into the future: me to my *Republic*, you to your *Armada*.

GREY AREAS

be careful who you love
and who you live above

be careful what you do
and who does what to you

be careful who you kiss –
a mouth can spit and hiss

be careful who you call
to stand inside your hall

be careful who you meet
upon a lonely street

be careful with that stray
at night all cats are grey

but please, please, please

be careful in your bed
with items pink or red

THE LUNG LAUNDERETTE

Waiting in the Pulmonary Function Suite
for my Myocardial Perfusion Scan,
I see the nurse clip my chest X-Ray
to a piece of string straddling a light box.

Gawping for ages, I try to decipher
the bar code of my ribs, the stacked cups
of my spine. And what of that grey nebula
hubbled in my pectus like a lethal gas?

I hold a spirit-level to it. Hang a plumb
line off it. Take a light-meter reading.
Spit on a Kleenex and rub, grab a brush
and scrub the smudge with Daz.

Speaking to my doctor a week later, he says
I'll have to retake the test; that cloudy
area was an error due to insufficient radiation
and not, as first suspected, something sinister.

I cancel the headstone carver,
inform the Minister.

ON CLIO LANE

Stade Geoffroy-Guichard.
St. Etienne.
Coupe Du Monde 1998.

Scotland v Morocco,
to my sorrow.

But I can't complain:
it was all sun, no rain.

We marched from the town
to the stadium,
a spare and Spartan
Tartan Army, singing –
We're polite and we know we are!

The locals lined the streets
as if to greet a liberating force.

One girl, leaning out of a window
high up a block of flats,
was greeted by five thousand
Scots (and me) chanting:

Nicole!
Nicole!

When she shouted back:

Papa!
Papa!

A thousand Scotsmen
ran for cover.

NEW CARGOES
After John Masefield

Wrinkle cream of Nivea from fragrant Oprah,
flowing foam of Radox at frothy bathing time,
with a carload of Opium, Avon and Comptoir,
Lagerfeld, L'Oreal, and Calvin Klein.

Spicy scented Givenchy splashing on at Christmas,
dipping through departments in the pristine stores,
with a chargecard for Demeter, Erreuno, Alchimie,
Trussardi, and Benetton, and Haute Couture.

Feisty British shopper with a dog-eared Switch Card
bustling through the beggars and the shopping drones,
with a cartload of cut price, marked down, shop-soiled,
Shell Suits, Reeboks and mobile phones.

BY GRAND CENTRAL STATION

I sat down and swept
the dust of our love
affair from the sleeves
of my coat and gathered
it up as the raw
material for a poem,
the novel having already
departed from platform
one with far too many
carriages, far too opulent,
clinging upholstery.

ON BIRDS

The thrush, pecking a hole in silence,
sings at the speed that sound attains
when a voice has wings.

The seagull, mourning in the trawler's wake,
inscribes a neat parabola, then tilts, top heavy
into a dart that punctures a lake.

The eagle saws a slice of sky that falls
to form its shadow, and the earth reflects
a feathered storm.

The hawk, the instructor of my eye, displays
with all its darting pace the deadly grace
of what it is to fly.

ON YOUR RADIO TONIGHT

Musicians are the world's timekeepers.
They're awake for all of late p.m. and early-middle a.m.

They invented, rented, syncopated time. In fact,
they own time, loaning it to our ears chord by chord.

Some would say they own our tears, conjuring
the moistness of memories with a single note.

Others would call them tyrants for invoking
the bliss of loss with a single stroke of a string.

Sneaking up on you, one will blow a note
of such melancholy it turns your heart to jelly.

They're the strummers, the drummers, the blowers:
we're the suckers for every plucker.

Dynamite to broken hearts, they sharpen solitude
to a needlepoint stuck in the vinyl groove of the past.

Turn the dial to left or right, there's no safe songs
on your radio tonight.

KLAONICA NOMENCLATURE

i) Arenas

Maracana, Latin America.
Stadio San Siro for Milanese.
The Comunale of Fiorentina.
The Velez Sarsfield of Argentina.
The Sapporo Dome of the Japanese.
El Estadio de Cartagena.

ii) Grounds

Reebok, Brunton, Ibrox, Fratton.
Glanford, Sixfields, Saltergate.
Dudgeon, Millmoor, Sincil Bank.
Ricoh, Bescot, Plaskynaston.
Stark's Park, Stangmore, Afan Lido.
Crabble, Tolka, Gortakeegan.

iii) Theatres

Gradski, Jelkic, Banja Luca,
Vukovar, Sarajevo, Tuzla,
Kosovo, Bosnia, Srebrenica.

iv) Occupations

Butcher, baker, ice cream maker,
Red Star Ultra, Balkan Tiger –
Arkan kicked off in Herzegovina.

SIXTEEN SLICES OF MY HEART

I'm wired with electrolytes,
strapped to the jackknife bed.

My hands hold opposing elbows above my head.
I'm raised towards the Gamma Scintillation Camera

and offered to the image slicer, which will snap
my heart from sixteen angles.

The radionuclides injected earlier are emitting rays,
exciting crystals in the arcing photo-heads above me.

Its *gamma glamour* pics will determine if the angles
and the angels are moribund or scintillant.

a haiku is like
an orange with seventeen
pips in three segments

skimming a pebble
across the soul-still water –
nine bridges of air

poor cold potatoes
not wanting to be eaten
keep their jackets on

some go to work on
buses, some take taxis but
poets hitchhaiku

a butterfly fell
into a dream of flowers –
your eyelids fluttered

winter deep and hard
sharp with brittle icicles
frost is finger-thick

oxymoronic
(good grief!) has five syllables!
(handy for haiku)

you don't need a high
i.q. to write a haiku –
just zen and paper

ERIC CANTONA MEETS FRIDA KAHLO

They always put the wheelchairs
behind the goals. That's how Frida
and I met. She was sketching me.

I was sketching your shirt. I love
the wantonness of that upturned collar.
I will use it for my next self-portrait.

We make things visible that are
not visible. I make goals out of nothing,
Frida makes many Fridas visible.

I don't get out much. Diego does
the cooking. I cover his murals
with mirrors. I paint what I see.

Remember my kung fu at the Palace?
When the merde hit the fan
you give me a Mexican wave.

It was a wave of dismissal. I'm bored
of petty Napoleons. Like the ball you kick,
you are just a bag of wind. Goodbye!

Au revoir to you, ma petite sardine!
Your eyebrows are like my drawing of
the seagulls that follow the trawler.

Do you know what they say about you, Eric?

Non, Frida.

Dicen que no le acertarias al culo de
una vaca ni con un banjo.

Pardon?

Un cul de vache. Un banjo.
Tu le manquerais par loin.

IN PRAISE OF HATRED

Goodbye to the cane, the belt and the buckle:
the duster, the ruler, the strap.

Goodbye to the hard-knocks with flick knives
and bike chains, fists full of chips off the old block.

Goodbye to the factories and the grinding machines:
the drill bit, the hacksaw, the rasp.

Adieu to you, all you teachers and foremen.
Fuck you so much for your sterling efforts.

Let us now stand and applaud our transgressors
for lending their spite and their bile to our lines,

for the slivers of steel they insert in our stanzas.
They also serve, who only snarl and bait.

DESIRED ERRATA

Dear Miss X,
There were several typographical errors in your recent
love letter to me. I return it to you for the necessary
*   amendments.*

For *we* read *me*
For *is* read *was*
For *you* read *who?*

For *love* read *shove*
For *cherish* read *perish*
For *wanton* read *wanting*

For *undying* read *denying*
For *breathless* read *lifeless*
For *sweetheart* read *faintheart*

For *infatuation* read *trepidation*
For *engagement* read *estrangement*
For *monogamy* read *monotony*

For *foreplay* read *beforeplay*
For *laughter* read *slaughter*
For *petting* read *forgetting*

For *panting* read *parting*
For *Eros* read *errors*
For *tongue* read *tied*

For *ring* read *sting*
For *you* read *her*
For *sex* read *ex*

Yours Unfaithfully,
Mr. Y

KENNETH'S FATHER'S CANINE IS DECEASED

Ken Dodd's Dad's Dog's Dead.

Dodd's Dog's Dead, Ken? – Dad.

Dad Dodd's Dog's Dead – Ken.

Dog's Dead? – Ken Dodd's Dad.

Dead – Ken Dodd's Dad's Dog.

PUBLISHED POET

If I was published
I'd get big-headed.
I'd strut and swank,
and look down
on clowns like you.
That's what I'd do.

If I was published,
I could ignore
my lack of lustre,
my shabby demeanour
and my dreary personality.

I would ask you not
to judge me on my looks
but on my covers –
the covers of my *books*.

If I was a published
sort of poet, I'd leave you
in no doubt about it
I'd shout it, spout it
out at parties:
I'm a PUBLISHED poet!

And you would be my…
well, my public:
the tracers of my phases
and my trends,
my readers, my awe-
dience, you who once
were merely my friends.

CYBER POET WANTED

Candidates must demonstrate a good
working knowledge of the following:

www (william wordsworth's writings).
URL (Understanding Robert Lowell).
ISP (Imitating Sylvia Plath).
JavaScript (John Ashbery's Very Astute Script).
HTML (How To Mutilate Language).
FTP (Forgot To Punctuate).
SCSI (Syllable Counting Speeds Insanity)
RAM (Renga Annuls Marriages)
FAQ (Frequently Altered Quatrains)
GIF (Ghazal-Induced Flatulence)

Experience of Enun-C8 and
Rhymeweaver 3.1 software essential.

The Residency will be for 101 years.
The Cyber Bard will be cryogenically
preserved by the sliver of ice in his/her heart
until the very last Arts Council has crumbled
beneath the weight of its own inertia.

Applications by e-mail, quill or telephone.
All cat-calls will be charged at local rate.

A PERFECT POEM

Look, I'm sorry.
I know I promised you a poem,
a perfect poem, on this very page.
It was here this morning.
But it's gone now.
Gone.

You would have loved it.
All the letters were heart-shaped
and the words were so tender
they looked like silver tears.
The page itself would tremble
like a handkerchief waving goodbye.

Yet the poem had teeth:
it was a sassy little number,
a street-wise, sardonic piece
with wit so sharp I cut my fingers
to shreds just writing it,

but it was ambitious,
and though it knew I loved it dearly,
no page of mine could ever hold it.

It wanted to be a star, you see.
Wanted to be published in anthologies,
to be set-reading for GCSEs,
be translated into Japanese,
and be read aloud by famous tongues
on *Poetry Please.*

The last time I saw it,
it had had enough.

This morning,
as I was leaving to meet you,
I passed it in the hallway.
It was on the phone
to Roger McGough.

THE MAGIC OF POETRY

Thank you for buying this
modest slim volume,
The Magic of Poetry.

I'm glad you persevered
as far as this page. After all,
I can't do this by myself.

You don't mind being a poet's
assistant for a moment, do you?

Good, then let us begin…

I'll take the top two corners
of the page while you grab
the bottom really tight.

Now pull with all your might!

Abracadabra!

Do you see what we've done?
Together we've got to the end
of the page without having
to suffer a single line of poetry.

No, please don't applaud.
It's the oldest trick in the book.

PUSHING UP DAISIES

The Librarian went Dewey-eyed
at the merest mention of verse.
But, sadly, she duly died
from the old anthology curse.

The ladder-slip, the top shelf gasp,
one hand held *The Time Traveler's Wife*,
the other one just failed to grasp
101 Poems That Could Save Your Life.

POEM &

Love, you say?
I've been there,
I've been down that low.

Life, you say?
I am there,
not too far to go.

This, I say, and this alone,
is what I've learned and know:

Hell is a fingerhold.

Heaven's letting go.

COUNTER POEM

Love, you say?
It touched me once,
sensuous and slow.

Life you say?
It's just a glance –
a wave before you go.

This, I say, and this alone,
is what I've learned and know:

Heaven is a fingerhold.

Hell is letting go.

CLEAR AND PRESENT ANGER

Let's put it this way:
you ignited, exploded, boiled over.
I tried to muffle, smother, mute it.
But my appeasement simply fuelled it.

You erupted like Krakatoa.
I was ice floe, hoarfrost,
glacier, pure refrigeration.
You were Fahrenheit, I was Kelvin.

You were molten throughout
the palaver, hot as a solar corona.
I was cat-calm, composed, serene
while you vented your spleen.

You fumed, flamed, blazed,
like you'd swallowed hot lead.
Come on – spit it out –
was it something I said?

COMING TO TERMS WITH IT

Perhaps in time maybe I will get used to it;
the Madeleines, the tea, the Marcel Proust of it,

though daily, constantly, I feel confused by it.
Your love, that absentee, I am bemused by it.

The koan, quark, the Rubik Cube and Johann Faust of it.
The trace, the evanescing shade, the Marley's Ghost of it.

My love, an amputee, has been abused by it.
My plea for clemency has been refused by it.

This is calamity: my heart is bruised by it.
I know, despite my plea, I'll be accused by it.

HOW THINGS ARE IN GLOCCA MORRA

Not so good these days. The brook is full
of minging mattresses and Tesco trolleys. It limps
down to Donny cove but it still runs through
Killybegs, Kilkerry and Kildare in case it gets mugged.

The willow tree was uprooted as part of the new 'Brook
Side Executive Detached Villas' housing development.
I'm afraid the lassie's twinkling eye has got a cataract
and she's on a year's NHS waiting list. She can't come

whistlin' by any more because she's out of Fixodent
and can't afford to buy a new tube, what with the twins
to feed on her measly Child Allowance and no money
being sent from that waster of a husband who's off

drinking and whoring for weeks on end, the focca.
The biggest focca in Glocca. Of course *she walks
away, sad and dreamy there not to see you there.* But she
couldn't see you if you jumped out at her. The cataract,

remember that? You can ask all the weeping willows
that you care, along with each and every bleeding brook
and whistling lass, that comes your way but none of them
will know, you ass, what the fuck you mean by *Tooralay.*

AT MELTING POINT

I am here and you are there.
Without you I am incomplete.
Perhaps the two of us should meet
at Melting Point in Golden Square.

I promise I will be discreet.
You'll hardly even know I'm there.
You say you might as well stay where?
At Freezing Point on Silver Street?

Let's meet at the Lemon Tree.
Last year I overlooked you there.
Or where the poets meet upstairs –
in Books and Beans, if you are free.

Please sit at that window seat
I walked straight past this time last year.
Tonight I won't be late, I swear.
Where's Freezing Point on Silver Street?

I am here and you are there.
Without you I am incomplete.
Now one of us, at least, should meet
at Melting Point in Golden Square.

IN MEMORIAM

Leaning against a winter wall,
Cemetery bus stop,
Great Western Road.

Ain't it cold, boys,
Ain't it cold?

The Wallis Girl
waltzing by
throws a glance
behind me to the graves,
then high-heels away.

No recognition
of my human condition,
the birth of breath on my lips,
my upright position.

Ain't it cold, boys?
Ain't it cold?

THE FORD'S PRAYER

Give us this day our daily stress.
And give unto those who stress against us
some of their own medicine,
which they so richly deserve.

Let us take to our cars in the morning
and in the evening, into the pique-hour traffic
and let us drive each other to the brink of violence.

Let us smart from signals of one finger
and of two fingers, and let us jerk these fingers
at the jerks who cut us up at traffic lights
and make us see red.

Let us gnash our teeth in disbelief at dickhead
antics of boy-racers who want to exit early
and take us with them into mayhem,
which is one of the states of Youth.

But let there also be tolerance of our own
shortcomings. Let us perfect our looks
in mirrors at sixty miles per hour
whilst chatting on our Motorolas.

And give us this day our daily stretch
of open road, except for the cyclist puffing
his way up the incline. And let the bastard
be grateful for a soft landing in the mud.

ANAPESTS

Don't take your kids to a poetry reading.
They fiddle, they twitch, need constantly feeding.

They fidget, they whimper, consistently mutter.
They're always thumping their sister or brother.

They're such a distraction to poetry readers
who secretly plot how to murder the bleeders.

It's difficult giving a flawless recital
when some snotty urchin cries at the vital

moment: it judders and jars like a misplaced
enjambment: it jang

les the nerves and scuppers the rhyme,
knocks the metre out of kilter

One bogey-flicker can spoil the whole thing.

Don't bring your kids.
Your kids – don't bring.

WIFE OF Pi

3.141592
but you don't stop there do you?

caring

nothing for brain cells burning
you greedy little sod (sorry for

swearing)

you've been to every decimal
place on Earth

deterring

other roaming numerals from

daring

you've grown too big
for you roots

inferring

someone ought to knock you
down a peg or two

recurring.

HENRI ROUSSEAU MEETS FRANK O'HARA

It's a jungle out there, Frank.

I know, Henri. Was it you
who brought all this humid
weather over from Brooklyn?

There are tigers roaming Central
Park. Don't go there at night without
a flashlight, a pitchfork and a net.

They say you left a naked girl
on a divan, smack in the middle
by that phallic obelisk, you brute.

Don't worry about the girl, Frank,
the saucer-eyed lions look after her.
Say, how long is your lunch break?

It's fluid as a Dali dial, Henri. Museums
have their midday naps. Hell, all that
time they cram in between the entrances

and exits. Nobody's clockwatching
in Antiquities. You fancy a papaya
and a jambalaya from Juliet's Corner?

Papaya? Jungle juice sounds just up
my street. I'd like to do you in oils, Frank,
peeking through a bush on Seventh Avenue.

AESOP'S FIELD

was advertised for a silver shilling.
It spread over numberless hectares
and stretched this buyer's incredulity,
so he requested an inventory.

He strode out in boots with pipe
and cane, and a wary countenance.

Perchance he passed a man bearing
a thorn, stroking the mane of a lion.

Further on he saw a tortoise astride
a white line, mere inches away
from a sleeping hare.

Later on, he came upon a well
with a goat at the bottom.

He noticed an army of angry ants
and a famished singing grasshopper.

He walked on, encouraged.

At the far end of the field he saw
a fox spitting out grapes.

When he heard an eagle cry *Alas!*
and saw a peacock carrying a petition,
he phoned the seller with an offer.

He had to agree, it was prime parable land.

LIGHT SNACK

My doctor said –
You're suffering from Night Starvation.

Midnight.
NASA reports
teeth marks on the moon.

FLAVOURS OF QUARK
(A Sub Atomic Mnemonic)

BOTTOMS *going*
UP *and*
DOWN *have a*
STRANGE
CHARM *that's tip –*
TOP.

ASCENT OF MAN

Resurrection Saturday.

Bloody Sunday.

Hiroshima Monday.

Twin Towers Tuesday.

Gagarin Wednesday.

Berlin Wall Thursday.

Dress-Down Friday.

I CHING TO GO

Stars are forming hexagrams
around a Yin Yang moon.
A night of possibilities!

INDELIBLE

Weeks after the wake,
my first dream of you.

You're standing at the rails of a ship
on a clear blue day, sailing on that huge
Cunarder we used to watch from the Pier
Head; decked out for a breezy jamboree,
floating towards an improbable country.

From your stillness you turn to me, say nothing,
but your eyes speak of fair weather and calm waters.

As the eighth bell tolls I leave you there
and swim back to wakefulness, viewing your
vast indelible smile from my far impossible shore.

GIN & MILTONIC

She was a victim
of the war
between the sexes –
the Yom Kippur
of fallen exes.

A waitress in a
Strip Joint, she raves –
guyless in Gaza,
by the till with knaves.

HALF OF A HALF-HEARD CONVERSATION PLUCKED OUT OF THE YELLOW HUM OF CABS AND CHATTER, DOWNTOWN MANHATTAN

…but God never said
Thou Shalt Be A Sucker.

IN JUNE

There's a sign on the moon saying
Closed For The Night.

Thank God! said the poet –
I'm too pissed to write.

OIL STATE

Seas of wealth below Kuwait.
Oil is money's liquid state.

OFF YER COAL FACE & CO.

His father sold coal, now he sells coke.
The old family business went up in smoke.

The son drives a Porsche, wears Gaultier clothes.
The new family business gets up his nose.

ANOTHER OVERSIGHT FROM NOAH

And then my sister, Rita, gets all melancholy
and she says to me:

You know what I wish, Eddie?

No I don't, Rita, what do you wish?

I wish I'd seen a unicorn before they became extinct.

AND THEN

And then there is
the stillness of trains –
the silence
at the core of a bullet

THE UNCERTAINTY PRINCIPAL

Or is it *principle?*

THE PERILS OF OVERSLEEPING

R.I.P.
Van Winkle.

ULURU

Ayers Rock
burning
in the Bush
like a solid
sunset

THE EVENING'S ALE

    EVEN
    -ING
    WILL
    COME
    THEY
    WILL
    KNOW
    THE
    NEW
    ALE

WHY LOVE HURTS

I think I know why
you're feeling stung and lost –

love is a butterfly
that mated with a wasp.

CONSOLATIONS

The first week over, I said to my sister:
Before we know it, it'll be a year.

Then we'll be placing anniversary flowers
in the garden of his memory.

Meanwhile, there's refuge in things
beyond his compass,

I drive to work knowing full well
that his hands never held a steering wheel,

or sit at my computer knowing he never
caressed a keyboard with his fingers.

I have come to know the small consolations
of technology:

mobile phones, e-mails, DVDs –
all safe from any taint of melancholy,

but football scores, gunfighter ballads,
darts, snooker, the *Grand Ole Opry,*

that's a different story.

RELICATESSEN

Aunty Consumptia was an avid collector
of Holy Relics and empty decanters.
Her doorbell chimed *Adeste Fidelis.*

A saint-embroidered carpet led to the lounge,
where a ceiling mural showed The Last Supper,
with Consumptia serving The Lamb
of God a nice hot cuppa.

Her parrot screeched the Lord's Prayer yea loud.
The bedrooms had mobiles of Jesus Revenant.
She had a tablet cupboard which she vowed
now housed the fabled Ark of the Covenant.

Ten Virgin Marys glowed in her cellar.
The shower had Martyr's Palmolive shampoo.
In the attic, two tanks full of Holy Water.
Thankful postcards from Lourdes lined the loo.

Me, Rosetta and Stephen Ignatius
journeyed each Christmas with Frankincense,
Myrrh and Terry's All Gold.

We never stayed long in aunty Con's house,
though we were hers to have and to scold.
She didn't like my agnostic sneer,
or Stephen's habit of getting stoned.
She didn't like Rosetta's tone.

She would watch us outside
through her Turin Shroud curtains,
get cross with us for causing a rumpus;
a holy show in front of the neighbours:
Mr & Mrs Thomas Aquinas.

WING NUT

This is a nut with knobs on:
a Mickey Mouse mimic,
confined to comic spirals.
Up and Down
are not in its diction,
they are functions
of circum-
locution.

It moves by rule
of thumb;
a twisted butterfly
fluttering on
unflappable
wings.

ANTE POST

When death visits one it visits many
to tell them all redemptions are foreclosed.

If death visits you it is your family
who linger while you're giving up the ghost.

Death is never pro-, it's always anti –
no dead-heat is ever diagnosed.

Death's guess is always on the money –
backing you to be first past the post.

FLIGHT OF GEESE

Translating V as a hieroglyph for flight,
Wing-sprung we gain exultant height.

Ascent is gift, is thrilling lift in air.
Aloof to fall, we trawl the *Where*.

When's ahead – beyond the beak's magnetic edge –
Why is found on night's dark ledge.

PANTOUM OF THE OPERA

Is this one *Wagner's Ring?*
There's a cycle in it somewhere.
We'll know the show is over
when the Fat Lady sings.

There's a cycle in it somewhere,
and the Nibelungen Ring.
When the Fat Lady sings
we'll drive to Götterdämmerung

down the Nibelungen ring road.
In a Norbert Dentressangle truck
we'll drive to Götterdämmerung.
Valkyries check their Vodafones

in a Norbert Dentressangle truck.
We'll know the show is over when
Valkyries check their Vodafones:
is this tone Wagner's ring?

RAIN ON THE FACTORY YARD

The skip, the drum, the blue container.
The drip, the thrum on the new step ladder.

Extractor fans like upturned snails.
Yellow-painted hazard rails.

Flowing water flooding drains.
Seagulls nest in ten-ton cranes.

Workmen trudging through the puddles,
smoking fags in soaking huddles.

Rainbow hues in oily pools.
Rivulets of leaking fuels.

Shoe treads slipping in the slime.
Raindrops hit bullseyes every time.

DEAN, SMITH & GRACE

A half-back line from pre-war Blackburn,
knee-length shorts and Dubbined boots?

Or a trio of solid sloggers clocking up the score
in a see-saw skirmish for the Ashes?

No, these were men who built brutes of machines,
though some would say they had an inner grace.

And tales were spawned among the tin-mug tribes
of that rarest Turner's prize – the Mile-Long Lathe.

One thousand tradesmen standing at their posts
would skim their yards of shaft with carbide tools.

While a hundred foremen tannoyed to their charges
when to index out and index in.

The shaft was held in place between two centres
and measured twenty feet around its rim.

Supports were placed at hundred-yard divisions
and sky hooks took the loading in between.

A solly oil Sargasso cooled the cuttings
and washed the tons of swarf into the sump.

Or so the legend went at teabreak talk-ins,
those blether regions of the factory floor.

The lads with any sense would leave the tradesmen
reeling out their yards and yards of yarn.

johnpaulgeorgeringo
pauljohnringogeorge
georgejohnpaulringo
ringopauljohngeorge
johnpaulringogeorge
pauljohngeorgeringo
georgejohnringopaul
ringopaulgeorgejohn
johngeorgepaulringo
paulgeorgeringojohn
georgepauljohnringo
ringojohnpaulgeorge
johngeorgeringopaul
paulringojohngeorge
georgepaulringojohn
ringojohngeorgepaul
johnringopaulgeorge
paulringogeorgejohn
georgeringopauljohn
ringogeorgejohnpaul
johnringogeorgepaul
paulgeorgejohnringo
georgeringojohnpaul
ringogeorgepauljohn

REASONS FOR WRITING

The day swells up
to flood me with breath.
I plunge into
the well of the world.

The day swells up
to trap me in time.
I'm caged within
the pendulous hours.

The day swells up
to shrink me with space.
I dwindle down
to angstrom dimensions.

The day swells up
to drown me in dross.
I throw myself
these life lines.

ABDICATION

Because dust coats the throat.
Because heat bakes the tongue.
Because a man, like a king,
needs an excuse for his domestic abdication,
I tie my dog by its leash
to a lamp post and enter the bar,
my own leash stretched to breaking point,
and lord it over my province of pints.

COUNTDOWN

You were five, ten years ago.
I held your hand up all the stairs,
counting every step to sleep.

I read you rhymes and Fairy Tales,
told you lies about the dark,
counting every step to sleep.

I numbered all the stars for you
but hid those numbers hard and true,
counting every step to sleep:

for every prince a thousand toads,
for every smile a thousand tears,
counting every step to sleep.

I turned around and went back down,
counting my remaining years,
counting every step to sleep.

FLOWER GIRLS

There were days when my father took me to town
to see the circus of the streets: hawkers, market stalls
and my aunties, the Flower Girls of Williamson Square.

They peeked like petunias from under their scarves,
wore shy smiles against the wind, fingered flowers through
sawn-off mittens, pocketed pennies, tanners and florins.

Then we wandered through fog to the Pier Head,
a vastness of slabs where slaves once shuffled
in chain-linked lines for auction in the Confederate States.

We came in saner times to see a white man in chains,
for amusement, not enslavement. Shackled head to foot,
upside-down in a sack, he won his freedom in seconds flat.

This was childhood folklore: the ghosts of Speke Hall,
the Childe of Hale, who was nine feet tall, the Witches
of Pendle: spectres that drove you to bolt your door.

And over my shoulder, some thirty miles eastwards,
a girl The Echo described as vivacious met someone
called Myra whilst picking flowers on Saddleworth Moor.

QUEST FOR MARS

Aboriginal astronomers Walkabout Australia.

Congolese oncologists combat Zulukaemia.

Chilean etymologists decipher Inca pictographs.

Mongol opthalmologists ogle Hubble holographs.

Algonquin uranologists discover Deep Field pulsars.

Scottish ingenuity develops deep-fried Mars bars.

HUMPTY FUCKING DUMPTY

Passing a mixed media object, 2390 x 3276 x 1067 mm, by Bill Woodrow, titled *English Heritage – Humpty Fucking Dumpty*, described by the artist as *A section through history*, I noticed items of female underwear scattered willy-nilly about the piece. Curious, I tippy-toed around the precarious structure, admiring as I did so its sections of a vaulting box, a wheeled plough, a book, a clocking-in machine and a box with radiation hazard markings, which to my mind symbolised human progress, and discovered at the rear a naked couple copulating, which to my mind symbolised human progression, in a very athletic and abandoned manner. I a-hemmed my presence to them, at which point they waved enthusiastically and shouted in unison: *Be with you shortly!* Not wishing to intrude on them any further, I moved on to admire the piece of heavily-guarded Blu-Tack that was the focus of the exhibition. Assuming it was an item from Picasso's Blu Period, I was about to walk over a pile of priceless abandoned bricks when I was summoned back to the mixed media object by the still-naked gatecrashers of the piece. We politely shook hands and I enquired about their presence behind the Humpdump display, to which the man replied: *We are the installation – I'm Humpty, meet Dumpty.*

DRINKING PARTNER

You're sitting alone, drinking.
Could be espresso,
could be cappuccino,
could be a cup of cold tears.

To avoid the eyes
of huddled couples
you place a sheet
of paper on the table.

A poem sidles up to you
and drinks your pen dry.

PERIDIOTIC TABLE

Element	*Properties*
Hydrogin	Drunkenness
Hellium	Damnation
Boreon	Tedium
Nightrogen	Darkness
Fagnesium	Coughing
Paluminium	Friendliness
Sillycon	Ridiculousness
Prospherus	Richness
Potatsium	Mashiness
Scandalum	Outrageousness
Titanicum	Disastrousness
Vainadium	Conceit
Mangonese	Fruityness
Zinc	See *Titanicum*
Arsenic	Bottom pinching
Bromine	Brotherliness
Krapton	Uselessness
Stropium	Awkward ness
Yttrium	Welshness
Antimoney	Hippydom
Idiodine	Stupidity
Xenon	Buddhixm
Noddymium	Childishness
Disturbium	Interruption
Erbium	Hesitation
Ytterbugium	Jiving
Osmondium	Donnyness
Aridium	Dryness
Bismuth	Mind your own
Plutonium	Cartoonish
Francium	Goes to Hollywoodium

ZERO GRAVITY

Sometimes a sound will stop you in your tracks:
an ice cream van, a fairground hum will waltz
you, fevered, back to that time you danced
to famous (now old-fashioned) songs.
Your fingers, stiffer now it seems,
tap the dashboard to a half-remembered tune.

Traffic lights flash their lazy Disco strobe.
Hazy slo-mo memories drift across your eyes.
The handbrake drops, not all the cogs engage.
You feel that zero gravity of age:
your life speeding forward
while your mind is in reverse.

I'VE TURNED INTO SIMON ARMITAGE

several times this week –
once on my moped, twice on my bike.

I tried to enj
amb him in between the spokes

but his spokesman pulled him
out again, told me to take a hike.

I've tried to copy Simon's style,
his crafty nips and tucks.

But I haven't got his knack.
I haven't got his looks.

I guess I'll just continue
pissing on his books.

CHANTS YOU RARELY HEAR

i)
German Bundesliga

We hate Bayern München
We hate Shalke too (they're scheiss!)
We hate Kaiserslautern
But Verein für Leibesübungen Borussia Mönchengladbach
we love you!

ii)
Dutch Eredivisie (NAC Breda)

If you hate
Nooit Opgeven Altijd Doorzetten Aangenaam Door Vermaak
En Nuttig Door Ontspanning Combinatie Breda
clap your hands.

If you hate
Nooit Opgeven Altijd Doorzetten Aangenaam Door Vermaak
En Nuttig Door Ontspanning Combinatie Breda
clap your hands.

If you hate
Nooit Opgeven Altijd Doorzetten Aangenaam Door Vermaak
En Nuttig Door Ontspanning Combinatie Breda.

Hate
Nooit Opgeven Altijd Doorzetten Aangenaam Door Vermaak
En Nuttig Door Ontspanning Combinatie Breda.

If you hate
Nooit Opgeven Altijd Doorzetten Aangenaam Door Vermaak
En Nuttig Door Ontspanning Combinatie Breda
clap your hands.

iii)
League of Anglesey

One
Clwb Pêl-droed Llanfairpwllgwyngyllgogerychwyrndrobwllllan
 tysiliogogogoch

There's only one
Clwb Pêl-droed Llanfairpwllgwyngyllgogerychwyrndrobwllllan
 tysiliogogogoch

One
Clwb Pêl-droed Llanfairpwllgwyngyllgogerychwyrndrobwllllan
 tysiliogogogoch

There's only one
Clwb Pêl-droed Llanfairpwllgwyngyllgogerychwyrndrobwllllan
 tysiliogogogoch

Thank Gogogogogod.

PAM AYRES MEETS ANDY WARHOL

I've got no Campbells on me shelf.
I prefers Knorr Cup-a-Soup, meself.
I wish I'd looked after me teeth.

Teeth are just too embarrassing for words.
Some people find fame embarrassing, Pam.
How many inches have been written about you?

A dozen prints of everything smacks of greed.
How many Marilyns does anyone need?
I wish I'd looked after me Wonderbra.

I feel attracted to you, especially as we've not met.
I'd love a date with your television. In fifteen
minutes everyone will be infamous..

I was famous once, now I'm famous once more.
I'd just stopped a mo' for me memopause.
I wish I'd looked after me dentures.

Death is just a department store for the soul.
Are you ready for the final Mall?
I am deeply superficial, in a spiritual way.

Now don't go getting morbid, Andy, me lad.
You've made a fortune since you've been dead.
I wish I'd looked after me muse.

Do you know what they say about you, Pam?

No, Andy, I don't.

They say you're a Diva, Pam, a Diva.

WHAT THEY SAY ABOUT YOU

They say that you'll be leaving me tonight.
I'm weary with remorse and loss of sleep.
I weep for all the things I can't put right.

The words we had were bitter, cutting deep,
my shamed averted eyes stare at the floor,
you gesture with a tired dismissive sweep.

You seem to be more distant than before –
a door to somewhere else now holds your gaze.
I raise my voice to supplicate, implore

for one more chance, a few forgiving days.
I touch your face and kiss a last goodnight.
The light is dimmed, the nurses walk away.

They say that you'll be leaving me tonight.

ARBEIT MACHT FREI

Twenty years ago
I set my foot in Dachau
I left a print in snow
and stopped to think of how
such places came to be

When I turned to go
I hoped I might somehow
free my thoughts, but no –
those words still escape me
now and now and now

DIVISION LINES

The train will divide at Dundee.

It will split into
those passengers
for Dundee
and those against
Dundee.

Those done with
Dundee (Un-Dees)
will occupy
the front three
carriages.

Those at the rear
(Pro-Dees) will
disembark

and avail themselves
of the dark delights
of the city's kirks.

Those in the sleeper
carriage (Nu-Dees)
can carry on
rear guardless.

CORNERS OF DESIRE
For and after Les Murray

New York City is blighted by numbers.
Midtown Manhattan is a gridlock of digits.
Oh, for a creeping Greenwich Village where
street names invade those numbing numerals.

Bring me my Map that will Unfold!
Bring me these Corners of Desire!

First and Firewater.
Second and Plantation.
Third and Depression.
Fourth and Prohibition.
Fifth and Amendment.
Sixth and Assassin.
Seventh and Insurgent.
Eighth and Rendition.
Ninth and Conspiracy.
Tenth and Impeachment.

All roads would lead to the Port (of) Authority
Bust Terminal, from where a constant stream
of dizzy blondes will take you to see the sites –

Wail Street.
Flattery Park.
Rump Tower.
Phoney Island.
Carneedy Hall.
Root Mean Square.
Statue of Flibberty.
Mighty Penn Station.
World Tirade Centre.

IN REMEMBRANCE OF ALOIS ALZHEIMER

Kraepelin gave your name to Presenile Dementia, that in-
famous disease which hangs like fog on the far horizon.

The Romans believed it was caused by reading
epitaphs on tombstones. Asians blamed it on phlegm

in the brain. Later, it was excessive humidity, though some
thought it was dryness. And for one brief day, aluminium.

Nissl's silver staining threw light into cells. His method
caused a sensation: Take the brain out. Put it on the desk,

then spit. When the spit dries, put the brain in alcohol.
Now alcohol ranks in the list of causes, though low, like

tobacco. And you, Alois, forgot twenty burning cigars,
one left at each of your students' microscope stations.

Reisberg's observation shows the coffin in the cradle;
the skull behind the cherub grin, the inability of skin

to recall all it was taut, the unretrievable thought, the brain
stormed (that part of you that doesn't want to be stroked).

The loss of acuity. You are your own worst memory.
The assassin in the genes killed the future and laid the past

to waste: your life story no longer a book, but a sentence.
Only forgetting will release you from regretting. Tangles

will untangle all the threads, render you alien to yourself
and your family. You'll meet them every day for the first

time: those strangers who speak of you as kin. You,
in your cuckoo skin. They will take you in & in & in.

They will never ever remember you.

THE BASHO STREET KIDS

in Basho Street School
Class 2B's room is silent
dinnertime of course

Fatty scoffs his chips
three bucketsful for starters
no fish in the lake

a Spotty object
lurks in the acne marshes –
a smelly leopard?

a skull and crossbones
Pieces of Hate for Teacher
Danny's pirate chant

what a handsome name:
Perciville Proudfoot Plugsley
he's still Plug ugly

black and blue jumpers
with black and blue eyes to match
twins Sydney and Toots

Cuthbert Cringeworthy
oh what a soppy swot!
somebody swat him!

that new kid Basho
writes sissy poems all day
cripes! what a girl's blouse!

IN THE OTHER DOLE QUEUE

I spot Yosser Hughes,
so I call to him –

Hey, Yosser!
What's it feel like
to be a fictional character?

Yosser shouts back –
I'm made up!

MERSEY MYTHS

The myth of the Liver Birds flapping their wings
whenever a virgin walks by.

The story that the female bird looks out to sea to see
if her seasick sailors are safe, while the male looks
towards the city to make sure the pubs are open.

The laugh about Ringo Starr being the best drummer
in the world, when he wasn't even the best drummer
in the Beatles.

The myth about Eleanor Rigby being buried near Father
McKenzie in a Woolton graveyard is open
to interpretation.

And the one about a William MacKenzie being buried
in a pyramid in Rodney Street churchyard, sat at a table,
playing cards, is closed to interpretation.

The myth that in Liverpool a Villanelle is a female
gangster.

There are no leprechauns playing bowls in Jubilee Park.

Springheeled Jack never jumped the queue at Woolies
to buy a Space Hopper and a Baby Bouncer.

There are no Jam Butty mines in Knotty Ash.
Mrs. Thatcher closed them down in 1983.

The myth about Adolf Hitler living with his brother
in Garston, attending Liverpool Art School
and in the register signing his christian name as *Heil.*

And that beauty about the monastery out at Norton
Priory housing the skull of Christ as a child.

The myth of my being a poet
because I once wrote a poem about myths.

DO NOT STAND AT MY GRAVE AND WEE

After Mary Elizabeth Frye-Up
To Simon Armitage

Do not stand at my grave and wee
It is not fair, why pee on me?
Was it that poem ten poems ago?
You are the yellow stains in snow.
I am all washed out and dead again.
You are the ceaseless pissing rain.

When you unbutton in the morning's bush
You are the swift, downpouring rush
Of torrents in their fluted flight.
I am the soft sod who died last night.
Do not stand at my grave and piss;
I am not there, I hope you miss.

THE UPTAKE

I figured it was over
when you didn't phone
for years on end.

IN THE MIDST OF GORILLAS

There were three of them
behind the glass, species
Gorilla gorilla gorilla!

Upset by their confinement,
my wife and daughter
wept and left.

We being of an ilk,
I stayed
and out-stared the Silverback.

HEARTS ON THE LEFT

I.M. Adrian Mitchell

i)
I was run over by your death one day
Ever since the ambulance I've talked this way –
You filled my mouth with laughter
Stroked my ears with silver
Lit my chin with buttercups
Snuffed my nose with peppermints
Strung my tongue with daisy chains
Rubbed my skin with women
Told me truths about Vietnam.

ii)
I met you once,
shook your hand.
Told you how your poems
shook my head.

iii)
I introduced myself
as one of those berks
not worthy to worship
the wheels of Eddy Merckx.

iv)
When they gave it to you ghostly,
did you give up the ghost?
Or simply slip away
while waiting for
the third opinion?

v)
When I'm sad and weary etc.,
I think of you
thinking about Celia
with nothing on.

(Celia with nothing on,
being thought about by you,
that is,
not you with nothing on,
thinking about Celia,
nor me with nothing on,
thinking about you
thinking about Celia,
that is.)

vi)
Poetic (i)
May I borrow your wheelbarrow?
Sorry, William Carlos Williams borrowed it
for wheeling wet chickens. He hopes it's dependable.

Paralytic
May I barrow your wheelborrow?

Poetic (ii)
May I borrow your wheelbarrow?
You ask for a wheelbarrow. *I offer you
a blade of grass.*

Poetic (iii) / Ballistic
May I borrow your wheelbarrow?
Here, wheelbarrow.

Spiritualistic
May I borrow your poem about a wheelbarrow?
Over my dead body…

FANAGRAMS

Emily Dickinson
Icy-minded icon in sickly mode.
No cosily inked melodic lines
in solemn dyke's idiom: likens all to nil.

Marilyn Monroe
A neon memory: Rimmel eye liner,
nylon élan; a romeo enroller (amor on amyl),
lay in a lonely room, a Miller memoir –
no Norma anymore.

Charles Bukowski
Sick lecher or slick hero?
No rosebush – he howls, wails, sulks.
Alehouse brawler; whore abuser who wrecks Buicks.
Raw oral shocker – he swears, bickers, bawls.
Biro-sucker slouch: cruel, bleak, crass.
A halo-hacker: his work kicks ass.

THE END OF POETRY

One of the secret powers of this poem
is to render the reader's clothing invisible.

This may account for the occasional
cries of alarm heard in Public Libraries.

So be careful where you read these words.
And next time you see someone bare

and oblivious in a bookshop stay calm.
Close the book and lead them gently

from the Poetry shelves, avoiding
the Children's section, and usher them

to the *Meet-the-Author* stand, where they will
join others to form a nude tableau entitled:

Reading Poetry Is Like Standing Naked In Front
Of People And Baring Your Soul To Them.

Let them become aware of each other's bodies.
Let them begin where all poems end.

YES, BUT WHAT ARE THE POEMS ABOUT?

To answer the question most frequently asked by
    interviewers:

EPILOGUE
Why should epilogues always be at the end of the book?
    Why do prologues get all the limelight?

Some of *Epilogue's* terms explained –
An *adjective* is a word whose main syntactic role is to
    modify a noun or pronoun, giving more information
    about the noun or pronoun's referent.
A *Sintactic* is a strategy that people employ to avoid
    being caught *in flagrante delicto*.
A *pronoun* is a professional noun. It is the mercenary in
    your dictionary.
An *abjective* is a word offering no hope whatsoever.
Alluding means *making a disguised reference to*. Always
    wear a mask when alluding.
Vocab is a sawn-off version of *vocabulary*, in the same
    way that constab is short for *constabulary* and *constant*
    stabbing.
Logo-language refers to the future reversion of words into
    symbols. *Texting* has begun this process.
*Metaphor*s – According to Old Armitage's Almanack,
    metaphors are things that arrive at station platforms.

BECAUSE I AM A POET
Avoirdupois mass. The Avoirdupois system is one of
    weights (or, properly, mass) based on a pound of
    sixteen ounces. *Auvoir Dupois* isn't French for weight
    loss, but it should be.
Wislawa Szymborska. Polish poet and translator, who
    was awarded the Nobel Prize for Literature in 1996,
    at the age of seventy-three. Szymborska is one of the
    few female poets to have received the prize.
STĘSKNIONY is Polish for *longing*.
Oranjeboom (Orange Tree) is a premium lager brewed
    in the Dutch town of Breda (See *Chants You Rarely*
    Hear.) An elegant, full-bodied lager, which balances
    a slight toffee maltiness with an apple-like fruitiness

and a lingering hoppy finish. Guaranteed to get you out of your tree.

BUDDHA'S GIRLFRIEND
Yes, Buddha had a girlfriend. It was a purely Platonic relationship, but nobody believed him because Plato had not been born and no one knew what the word meant. Maybe he sent a body double home while he was practising not-galavanting with Shirley in the temple. His wife spread his surrogate's butties with *I Can't Believe It's Not Buddha.*

WORD FOR WINDOWS
Q. What do you call a man with a sander in Liverpool?
A. The window cleaner.

AT THE JACQUES BOUTIQUE
Boutique – A boutique, from the French word for shop, is a small shopping outlet, especially one that specialises in elite and fashionable items such as clothing, jewellery and edible poetry books.
Fashion – It is highly unfashionable to attempt to define fashion.
Atkins – The Atkins Diet is a revolutionary weight loss technique conceived by the guitarist, Chet Atkins. His theory that food should not be eaten with a shovel and washed down with three bottles of red-eye whisky but should be picked at like a guitar string caused a sensation in Nashville. Overnight, overweight Country stars lost pounds of ugly flab either by getting divorced or by the simple practice of picking at their food. Many who got stuck in the doorway of the *Country Hall of Fame* found that Chet held the key. Careers were relaunched by newly-thin cowboys and crooners. Artists formerly known as Mince, Jah Wobble, Ernest Tubb, Fats Domino, Larry Lardarse and Pig Belly changed their names to Slim Whitman, Tiny Tim, Slim Pickens, Thin Lizzie and Slim Volume. Unfortunately, word of the Atkins diet didn't get through to Graceland, and Mr. Presley never did return to slender.

THE ELECTRODE LESS TRAVELLED
A real spine-tingler, revealing the shocking truth about
   the NHS (Non-Healing Service), and Ulrika Jonsson.
   You have a right to know.

THE DOWNSIDE OF KNOWING A POET
Ha! ha! ha! – as if there's an upside.

STANDING OUTSIDE THE BERG ROOM IN
   NEW YORK PUBLIC LIBRARY, HAVING BEEN
   REFUSED ENTRY, I CONTEMPLATE THE
   WORKS OF PAUL VIOLI
Room 320, The New York Public Library, Fifth Avenue
   and 42nd Street. New York, NY 10018-2788 (212)
   930-0802. The Berg Collection contains some 30,000
   printed volumes, pamphlets, and broadsides, and
   2000 linear feet of literary archives and manuscripts,
   representing the work of more than 400 authors. But it
   is of no use whatsoever to you if you are not allowed in.

A CALENDAR MONTH
Based on the *Greg or Ian* calendar, named after either
   Pope Gregory XIII or Ian of Arimathea, depending
   on whether you've consulted the papal bull of
   February 1582, or if you've read the Pay Pal bullshit
   of 2002, which credited Ian of Arimathea's Shopping
   Basket with $350 million for refusing to accept the
   Pope's edict that 15th October should immediately
   follow 4th October, thus depriving retailers of 10
   shopping days income per year, every year since
   1583. An easy test to check if you are on the Greg
   calendar is to book your holidays between the 5th and
   14th October and see what doesn't happen.
Regarding calendar girls, it is widely believed that the
   Knights Templar invented the practice of placing
   paintings of naked females above their locker
   calendars. When fighting away from home, these
   knights packed their calendars as cruise aids for use
   in those boozy bazaars on lonely Templar nights.

OUT OF THE BLUE
An ornithological poem about logical orniths.

ON NOT RUNNING OVER A FOX OR A DEER ON
    A LONELY ROAD AT NIGHT
No animals were sadistically mutilated and left to die in
    agony at the side of a road during the construction of
    this poem.

EPMTY NOW GWROS ERVEY BED
Based on a scientific study that states you can vastly alter
    the order of the letters in written words and they can
    still be understood. Is that corretc?

ABYSSAL
A writers' workshop kind of poem. You are required to
    stroke your chin and nod sagely after finishing this
    piece. You are then free to go. But only when told to
    do so!

MAGNUM HOPELESS
The author really did grow up in an area known as *The
    Poets,* though there's nothing very poetic about St.
    John's Estate in Huyton, Liverpool, home of Joey
    Barton. Stevie Gerrard was born on the Blue Bell
    estate, just a studs-up, two-footed, surgery-inducing
    tackle away from Joey.
The Emperor of Ice Cream is the title of a poem by
    Wallace Stevens.

IN THE GREEN ROOM
Michael Donaghy died just a few months after this
    event.

GREY AREAS
The *items pink or red* are, of course, hot water bottles.

NEW CARGOES
Borrowed from Masefield and souped-up with go-faster
    stripes.
John Edward Masefield was Poet Laureate from 1930 until
    his death in 1967. He is celebrated as the author of
    the classic children's novels *The Midnight Folk* and *The
    Box of Delights.*

ON BIRDS
Hope isn't the thing with feathers – a budgie is.

ON YOUR RADIO TONIGHT
Lying in your darkened bedroom listening to the radio
    with only your Dansette, your tranny, a flashlight and
    Pan's People to keep you warm.

KLAONICA NOMENCLATURE
The word *Klaonica* means slaughterhouse, butchery,
    shambles, in Serbo-Croatian. This poem started as
    a list of football stadiums, grouped by the music,
    or lack of it, in their names. I came across a list of
    stadiums in the Balkan countries. Many familiar
    newsreel names cropped up, including Arkan, the
    infamous Serbian warlord, who was leader of the
    Red Star Belgrade Tigers. *The Butcher of Bosnia*, as he
    is known, owned a bakery and an ice cream van. He
    drove a pink Cadillac. Arkan's birthname was Željko
    Ražnatović. He was gunned down in the lobby of a
    Belgrade hotel in January 2000.

A HAIKU IS LIKE
Haiku are numerically-challenged poems that can't
    count beyond seventeen. Literature's equivalent
    of the doodle, they are a doddle; the easiest poems
    on earth to produce, taking about 3 minutes each,
    including switching the computer on, opening
    WORD, writing the haiku and printing it.

ERIC CANTONA MEETS FRIDA KAHLO
Lowbrow meets eyebrow. Browse around this poem at
    your leisure.
Thanks to Irene Martinez for the Spanish translation.

DESIRED ERRATA
Always check love letters you receive for spelling mistakes.
    Correct punctuation is the primary prerequisite for a
    fulfilling relationship. *Good between the sheets* means
    something quite different to poets than it does to
    civilians. A misplaced apostrophe can lead to anxiety,
    apoplexy and swift endings to relationship's.

POEM &
Never buy poems across the counter unless you are
    accompanied by an irresponsible adult who should
    know better.

COUNTER POEM
In reality, this is an under the counter poem.

COMING TO TERMS WITH IT
You will have to come to terms with every line ending in
    it.

AT MELTING POINT
The poetry equivalent of Google Maps' Street View,
    showing various Aberdeen venues.

IN MEMORIAM
A winter's day in North East Scotland that makes
    Adlestrop look like a knees-up.

ANAPESTS
The Public Library is NOT a crèche! Poetry is a very
    precious thing written by extremely intelligent and
    sensitive individuals who may have been published
    and won prizes. They do not like to speak at lecterns
    which have been smeared with SNOT.

WIFE OF PI
The perils of marriage to a recurring number. The
    calculation of the digits of π has occupied
    mathematicians since the day of the Rhind papyrus
    (1500 BC). Ludolph van Ceulen spent much of
    his life calculating π to 35 places. Although he did
    not live to publish his result, it was inscribed on his
    gravestone. His biography *Me, I Ate All the Pi's* is an
    Amazon best-seller. The calculation of π also figures
    in the Season 2 *Star Trek* episode *Wolf in the Fold*
    (1967), in which Captain Kirk and Mr. Spock force
    an evil entity (composed of pure energy which feeds
    on fear) out of the starship *Enterprise*'s computer by
    commanding the computer to *compute to the last digit
    the value of pi*, thus sending the computer into an

infinite loop. Attendees at poetry readings will be familiar with the infinite loop concept. It is often accompanied by low moaning noises and gentle snoring. The only way to break the loop is to set the Dogs of Waugh on the reader.

HENRI ROUSSEAU MEETS FRANK O'HARA
This poem was inspired by Rousseau's painting *The Dream* which is held in the Museum of Modern Art (MOMA) in New York City. The poem was awarded a prize at the Inaugural Edwin Morgan International Poetry Competition, 2008. Frank O'Hara was a New York poet.

FLAVOURS OF QUARK
A sub-atomic mnemonic, listing the parts, known as *flavours,* of quarks.
The six different flavours are: *up, down, charm, strange, top* and *bottom.*
Quarks are reputed to be named after the phrase *Three Quarks for Muster Mark* in James Joyce's *Finnegan's Wake*

ASCENT OF MAN
Landmarks in evolution, concluding with the pinnacle of human self-determination – wearing jeans in work on Fridays. Not to be confused with the Hollywood Blockbuster – *Ascent of A Woman.*

GIN & MILTONIC
Reworking of a ditty by Milton. That's John Milton, not Milton Balgoni, though I am forever mixing those blokes up.

IN JUNE
This is the tenth rendering of this poem. It is currently undergoing a version therapy.

ANOTHER OVERSIGHT FROM NOAH
A *Save an Endangered Mythical Species* poem that came too late.

THE UNCERTAINTY PRINCIPAL
Heisenberg becomes the latest victim of a typographic
  erorr.

THE PERILS OF OVERSLEEPING
Rip Van Winkle is a short story by the American author
  Washington Irving, who also wrote *The Legend of
  Sleepy Hollow* and *Little Britain.*
Rip Van Winkle is not related to Rip Torn, Rip Tide,
  Rip Cord, Rip Saw, Rip Off, Rip Ository or Rip Rip
  Hooray. Nor is he related to Van Gogh, Van Guard,
  Van Hire, Van Morrison, Van Allen Belt, Van Der
  Sar or Van Slanzar de Fanel. No way is he related
  to Twinkle, Wankel, Perry Winkle, Tiggy Winkle,
  Sting Winkle, Winkle Pickers, Vanilla Ice, Wink
  Martindale or Ice Wink.

THE EVENING'S ALE
Based on THE EVENING SAIL by Ian Hamilton
  Findlay. Nothing, but nothing, is sacred in this little
  chapel of words.

WHY LOVE HURTS
An epic tale of romance and entymology. Covers the
  whole gamut from Rhopalocera to Lissopimpla.

CONSOLATIONS
An Elegy Written in a Country and Western
  Churchyard.

RELICATESSEN
Strange as it may seem, this is not a true story.

WING NUT
Hats off to The Author for tackling one of life's Great
  Themes!

ANTE POST
The safest bet you'll ever get from the Tic Tac man.

FLIGHT OF GEESE
A latter day Goosey Goosey Gander.

PANTOUM OF THE OPERA

The poem is the first in the English Language to translate Wagner's Ring Cycle (*Der Ring des Nibelungen)* into Queen's Scouse. A full performance of the poem will take place over four nights of open mic, during *Wordfringe 2010* at Books & Beans, Belmont Street, Aberdeen, with a total reading time of about 15 hours, depending on the poet's pacing. The first and shortest stanza, *Das Rheingold, Dat Is,* typically lasts two and a half hours, while the final and longest, *I've Götterdämmerung and I'm Buggered if I'll Let You Have a Bite,* is a five-hour performance – a masterpiece of brevity for open mic. A *pantoum* is a form of poetry similar to a villanelle. It is composed of a series of quatrains; the second and fourth lines of each stanza are repeated as the first and third lines of the next. This pattern continues for any number of stanzas, except for the final stanza, which differs in the repeating pattern. The first and third lines of the last stanza are the second and fourth of the penultimate; the first line of the poem is the last line of the final stanza, and the third line of the first stanza is the second of the final. Ideally, the meaning of lines shifts when they are repeated although the words remain exactly the same: this can be done by shifting punctuation, punning, or simply recontextualizing. And you thought writing a poem was a piece of piss, eh?

RAIN ON THE FACTORY YARD

It's the yard outside an office in Dyce, Aberdeen, where it has rained every day for the last six years.

DEAN SMITH & GRACE

It's about a lathe manufactured by a company called Dean, Smith and Grace. A lathe is a machine. A lathe operator is called a *turner*. *Solly oil* is a term for soluble oil. *Skyhooks* are a means of hooking loads onto clouds.

REASONS FOR WRITING

What you get when there's no footy on telly. An angstrom is one ten-billionth of a Metre.

ABDICATION

Before you cut loose,
put dogs on the list
of difficult things to lose…
Simon Armitage

Abdication is about a bloke walking his dog and nipping
into his local for a pint.
Which begs the question – what is it with blokes and
dogs? Is it because blokes wish they could do what
dogs do and get away with it? Is it because dogs wish
they could sit in the armchair smoking a fag and
glugging a Guinness?

COUNTDOWN

No, it's nothing to do with the TV series, though it does
contain some vowels and consonants. Not as many
as Vorderman, though.

FLOWER GIRLS

Their names were Joan Wynn and the Flynn twins.
Speke Hall is said to be haunted. It certainly feels
spooky. The Childe of Hale was John Middleton,
who was born in Hale village in Cheshire in 1578.
He grew to be 9 foot 3 inches.
The *12 Pendle Witches* were charged in 1612 with
murdering 10 people in and around the Pendle
Hill area of Lancashire by the use of witchcraft.
Guilty, M'lud! The author first encountered the word
vivacious in the Liverpool Echo, describing one of the
Moors murder victims.

QUEST FOR MARS

Every Slim Volume needs an Obscure Poem to make
the reader think the poet is a Really Deep Thinker,
thus ensuring that he/she will be invited to read at
Poetry Festivals. Mentioning Mars Bars also gives
the impression that the author is also a Really Deep
Fryer.

PERIDIOTIC TABLE
An idiot's guide to the Periodic Table. A truly symbolic
  piece.

IN REMEMBRANCE OF ALOIS ALZHEIMER
A truly memorable poem.

PAM AYERS MEETS ANDY WARHOL
A marriage made in Art & Poetry Heaven. Feel free
  to make endless Gestetner prints of this poem.
  Pam Ayers, MBE, is probably the most fitting Poet
  Laureate we never had. Did any other Laureate
  ever read at a Royal Variety Performance at the
  London Palladium? Then again at a Royal Gala
  Charity Reception in St. James's Palace, attended by
  HM (Helen Mirren) The Queen? How many times
  did Alfred Lord Tennyson appear on telly? Did
  Edmund Spenser ever have his own radio show? Did
  Wordsworth ever open a Woolworths? And what of
  Colley Cibber? A made-up name if ever there was!
  Did Nahum Tate ever win Opportunity Knocks?
  Admit it, Pam is, without doubt, the People's Poet.
  No disrespect to Carol Ann Duffy, but Pam really
  should be odds on favourite to take over from The
  Duffer as the next Fry & Laurieate. A Timeshare
  between The Pamster and John Cooper Clark would
  constitute a Poetry Dream Team.
Footnote: Ben Johnson was disqualified from the
  Laureateship for taking Anapestic steroids.

CORNERS OF DESIRE
Inspired by Les Murray's *Reclaim the Sites*. This tribute
  was written in Fredy's Iron Bar, corner of Fifth and
  Amendment, New Yank City.

I'VE TURNED INTO SIMON ARMITAGE
The author and *Armo* have so much in common it HAD
  to happen one day.
In many societies, urinating on poetry books is
  considered to be a compliment to the author. It
  is in fact an act of *liquid* homage, inasmuch as it
  implies an attempt to render the book unburnable,

thus preserving it for posterity. Posterity in a
public urinal, granted, but a better fate than befell
millions of books during the Thatcher Era, when
the wholesale closure of mines caused a Fossil Fuel
Crisis resulting in the entire population of *This
Septic Isle* burning all unwanted paper products in an
attempt to supplement the daily ration of one lump
of coal per day per household (per street in Scotland,
Northern Ireland and Welsh Wales). Only poetry
books with a high reader urine additive survived.

THE BASHO STREET KIDS
A series of haiku stuck together with pieces of old
    chewing gum.

IN THE OTHER DOLE QUEUE
A short conversation with Yosser Hughes, of *The Boys
    From the Black Stuff* fame. In Liverpool, every bloke
    named Hughes is called Yosser. The birds, of course,
    are called Yossette.
Yosser is an invention of Alan Bleasdale, who, funnily
    enough, also comes from Huyton, or Huyton-with-
    Robbery, as it is formally known.

None of the preceding poems have appeared in any of the following publications:

The Low Horse, Smith's Knob, The Wide Shirt, New Wittering Scotland, Pottery Review, Cencrusties, Chipman, Itch, Wet Coats Magazine, Gritting Teeth, Ironing, The Morefrog Papers, Anaesthesia, AcuMental, Get Lost, The New Porker, Orbit, The Backward Book of Poetry, Armpit, Joe Canoe's Soap, Tedium, A Gender, Bloody Liar, Blithe Spit, Ibid Tenquid, The Minging Muse, Mslesbia, New Dope International, The Damp Patch, The Times Lottery Supplement, Strides, Stop Wasting My Time, Amish Rake Fight, Five Fags Left, Yet Another Sarcastic Editor, The Steaming Pile, The Ill Quill, Rejection Skip, The Portaloo Poets, Fictional Royalties.

Eddie Gibbons moved from Liverpool to Aberdeen in a previous century. He was a prizewinner in the Inaugural Edwin Morgan International Poetry Competition, 2008. He has given readings in Berlin (for the British Council), Dortmund, New York, London (Bloomsbury Theatre and The Poetry Café), at the Edinburgh International Book Festival, the Edinburgh Fringe and StAnza (Scotland's International Poetry Festival). His work has been broadcast and published in magazines, including Quadrant Magazine, Australia.